The Complete Diabetic Cookbook for Beginners

Your Essential Guide to Navigating Diabetes with Flavor-Packed Meals and Expert Insights

Jarrell Knox

The Complete Diabetic Cookbook for Beginners
© Copyright 2024 by Jarrell Knox
All rights reserved

This document is geared towards providing exact and reliable information with regards to the topic and issue covered. The publication is sold with the idea that the publisher is not required to render accounting, officially permitted, or otherwise, qualified services. If advice is necessary, legal or professional, a practiced individual in the profession should be ordered. From a Declaration of Principles which was accepted and approved equally by a Committee of the American Bar Association and a Committee of Publishers and Associations. In no way is it legal to reproduce, duplicate, or transmit any part of this document in either electronic means or in printed format. Recording of this publication is strictly prohibited and any storage of this document is not allowed unless with written permission from the publisher.

All rights reserved.

The information provided herein is stated to be truthful and consistent, in that any liability, in terms of inattention or otherwise, by any usage or abuse of any policies, processes, or directions contained within is the solitary and utter responsibility of the recipient reader. Under no circumstances will any legal responsibility or blame be held against the publisher for any reparation, damages, or monetary loss due to the information herein, either directly or indirectly. Respective authors own all copyrights not held by the publisher. The information herein is offered for informational purposes solely, and is universal as so. The presentation of the information is without contract or any type of guarantee assurance. The trademarks that are used are without any consent, and the publication of the trademark is without permission or backing by the trademark owner. All trademarks and brands within this book are for clarifying purposes only and are the owned by the owners themselves, not affiliated with this document.

TABLE OF CONTENTS

CHAPTER 1: UNDERSTANDING DIABETES 1
Types of Diabetes 1

Symptoms and Risk Factors 2

The Importance of a Diabetic Diet 4

Myths and Misconceptions about Diabetes 5

CHAPTER 2: BUILDING A DIABETIC-FRIENDLY KITCHEN 9
Essential Kitchen Tools and Equipment 9

Stocking a Diabetic-Friendly Pantry 10

Reading and Understanding Nutrition Labels 12

Meal Planning and Preparation Tips 13

CHAPTER 3: BREAKFAST DELIGHTS 17
Overnight Oats and Chia Puddings 17

Savory Breakfast Skillets 18

Diabetes-Friendly Pancakes and Waffles 20

Smoothies and Juices 21

Egg-cellent Dishes 23

CHAPTER 4: NUTRITIOUS LUNCHES AND LIGHT MEALS 27
Wholesome Salads and Grain Bowls 27

Soups and Stews for All Seasons 28

Sandwiches and Wraps 30

Light Pasta and Rice Dishes 31

CHAPTER 5: SATISFYING DINNERS 35
Lean Protein Mains 35

Veggie-Packed Sides 37

    One-Pot and Casserole Meals 39

    Ethnic and Cultural Cuisines 40

CHAPTER 6: GUILT-FREE SNACKS AND TREATS 43

    Crunchy and Savory Snacks 43

    Fresh Fruit Desserts 44

    Diabetic-Friendly Baked Goods 46

    Frozen Treats and Smoothies 48

CHAPTER 7: BEVERAGES AND LIQUID REFRESHMENTS 51

    Infused Waters and Teas 51

    Smoothies and Shakes 53

    Mocktails and Cocktails 54

CHAPTER 8: COOKING FOR SPECIAL OCCASIONS 59

    Holiday Feasts and Gatherings 59

    Celebrations and Parties 60

    Game Day Bites 62

CHAPTER 9: MEAL PLANNING AND LIFESTYLE TIPS 65

    Creating a Balanced Plate 65

    Portion Control Strategies 66

    Exercise and Activity Recommendations 69

    Managing Stress and Emotional Eating 70

AUDIOBOOK: 3 EBOOK BONUS 75

AUTHOR BIO: JARRELL KNOX 77

CHAPTER 1

UNDERSTANDING DIABETES

Types of Diabetes

Diabetes is a chronic condition that affects how the body processes glucose, a type of sugar obtained from the food we eat. There are several types of diabetes, each with its own unique characteristics and causes. Understanding the different types is crucial for managing the condition effectively and maintaining overall health.

Type 1 diabetes: This type of diabetes is an autoimmune disorder in which the body's immune system mistakenly attacks and destroys the insulin-producing beta cells in the pancreas. As a result, the body is unable to produce insulin, a hormone that regulates blood sugar levels. People with type 1 diabetes must rely on daily insulin injections or an insulin pump to regulate their blood sugar levels. This type of diabetes typically develops in childhood or adolescence but can occur at any age.

- Type 2 Diabetes: Type 2 diabetes is the most common form of the disease, accounting for around 90% of all diabetes cases. In this type, the body either does not produce enough insulin or becomes resistant to its effects, resulting in elevated blood sugar levels. Unlike type 1 diabetes, type 2 is often associated with lifestyle factors such as obesity, a lack of physical activity, and an unhealthy diet. It typically develops in adulthood, although an increasing number of children and adolescents are being diagnosed with type 2 diabetes due to rising obesity rates.

- Gestational diabetes: This type of diabetes develops during pregnancy and generally resolves after giving birth. It occurs when the hormones produced during pregnancy interfere with the body's ability to use insulin effectively. Gestational diabetes can lead to complications for both the mother and the baby if not managed properly. Women who have had gestational diabetes are at an increased risk of developing type 2 diabetes later in life.

- Prediabetes: Prediabetes is a condition characterized by higher-than-normal blood sugar levels, but not high enough to be classified as type 2 diabetes. Without lifestyle changes or medical intervention, prediabetes often progresses to type 2 diabetes. However, with proper diet, exercise, and weight management, it is possible to delay or prevent the development of type 2 diabetes.

- Other Types: There are also less common types of diabetes, such as monogenic diabetes, which is caused by a single gene mutation, and secondary diabetes, which can result from other medical conditions or medications.

It is essential to understand the specific type of diabetes one has, as the management and treatment approaches may vary. Regular monitoring of blood sugar levels, following a balanced diet, engaging in physical activity, and adhering to prescribed medication or insulin therapy are crucial steps in managing any type of diabetes effectively.

Symptoms and Risk Factors

Diabetes is a chronic condition that affects how the body processes glucose, a type of sugar derived from the food we consume. Understanding the symptoms and risk factors associated with diabetes is crucial for early detection and effective management of the disease. This section will provide an in-depth exploration of the various signs and risk factors to watch out for.

One of the most common symptoms of diabetes is increased thirst and frequent urination. When glucose levels in the blood are high, the body attempts to flush out the excess sugar through urine, leading to dehydration and excessive thirst. Fatigue and lethargy are also common signs, as the body's cells are unable to effectively utilize glucose for energy production.

Another telltale symptom is blurred vision. High blood sugar levels can cause the lenses of the eyes to swell, leading to temporary vision problems. Additionally, some individuals may experience slow-healing cuts or bruises, as elevated glucose levels can impair the body's ability to heal properly.

Unexplained weight loss is another potential symptom, particularly in cases of undiagnosed type 1 diabetes. When the body lacks insulin, it cannot utilize glucose for energy, leading to the breakdown of fat and muscle for fuel, resulting in unintentional weight loss.

It's important to note that some individuals may experience no symptoms at all, particularly in the early stages of type 2 diabetes, making regular screening and checkups essential for early detection.

Regarding risk factors, genetics play a significant role. Having a family history of diabetes, particularly among close relatives such as parents or siblings, increases an individual's likelihood of developing the condition. Additionally, certain ethnic backgrounds, such as African American, Hispanic/Latino, American Indian, and Pacific Islander, are at a higher risk due to a combination of genetic and environmental factors.

Obesity and a sedentary lifestyle are also major risk factors for type 2 diabetes. Excess body weight, particularly around the abdominal area, can contribute to insulin resistance, making it harder for the body to effectively utilize glucose. Regular physical activity and maintaining a healthy weight can help mitigate this risk.

Age is another factor to consider, as the risk of developing type 2 diabetes increases with advancing age, particularly after the age of 45. Additionally, women who have experienced gestational diabetes during pregnancy or have given birth to a baby weighing over 9 pounds are at an elevated risk for developing type 2 diabetes later in life.

High blood pressure, abnormal cholesterol levels, and a history of cardiovascular disease are also associated with an increased risk of developing diabetes. These conditions are often linked to insulin resistance and can amplify the negative effects of diabetes on the body.

By being aware of these symptoms and risk factors, individuals can take proactive steps to detect diabetes early and seek appropriate medical attention. Regular check-ups, lifestyle modifications, and proper management can significantly improve the overall health and well-being of those living with diabetes.

The Importance of a Diabetic Diet

A diabetic diet is crucial for individuals with diabetes to maintain healthy blood sugar levels and prevent or manage complications associated with the condition. By adhering to a balanced and nutrient-rich eating plan, diabetics can improve their overall well-being and quality of life.

One of the primary objectives of a diabetic diet is to regulate blood sugar levels. This involves carefully monitoring carbohydrate intake, as carbohydrates directly impact blood glucose levels. It's essential to choose complex carbohydrates found in whole grains, fruits, vegetables, and legumes, as they are broken down more slowly and provide a steady release of energy. Limiting simple carbohydrates from sources like sugary drinks, sweets, and refined grains is also recommended.

Fiber plays a vital role in a diabetic diet. High-fiber foods help slow down the absorption of sugar into the bloodstream, preventing sudden spikes in blood glucose levels. Excellent sources of fiber include whole grains, fruits, vegetables, nuts, and seeds. Incorporating these foods into meals and snacks can promote a sense of fullness, aid in weight management, and improve overall digestive health.

Protein is another essential component of a diabetic diet. Lean proteins from sources such as poultry, fish, eggs, tofu, and low-fat dairy products can help maintain stable blood sugar levels and support muscle growth and repair. When combined with fiber-rich carbohydrates and healthy fats, protein can contribute to a feeling of satiety, reducing the temptation for unhealthy snacking.

Healthy fats are also crucial for individuals with diabetes. Monounsaturated and polyunsaturated fats found in foods like avocados, nuts, seeds, and fatty fish can improve cholesterol levels and reduce the risk of heart disease, a common complication of diabetes. However, it's important to limit saturated and trans fats, which can be found in processed foods, fried items, and some baked goods.

Hydration is another vital aspect of a diabetic diet. Drinking plenty of water and choosing beverages without added sugars can help maintain proper bodily functions, regulate blood sugar levels, and prevent dehydration, a potential risk factor for developing complications.

In addition to the dietary recommendations, portion control and meal planning are essential for effective diabetes management. Working with a registered dietitian or certified diabetes educator can help individuals develop personalized meal plans that take into account their specific needs, preferences, and lifestyle factors.

By embracing a diabetic diet rich in nutrient-dense foods, individuals with diabetes can take an active role in managing their condition, reducing the risk of complications, and improving their overall health and well-being.

Myths and Misconceptions about Diabetes

Diabetes is a chronic condition that affects millions of people worldwide, yet it is often shrouded in myths and misconceptions that can lead to confusion and misunderstanding.

Myth: Diabetes is caused by eating too much sugar.

While consuming excessive amounts of sugar can contribute to weight gain and increase the risk of developing type 2 diabetes, it is not the sole cause of the condition. Diabetes is a complex metabolic disorder influenced by various factors, including genetics, lifestyle, and environmental factors. Even individuals who consume minimal amounts of sugar can develop diabetes if they have other risk factors, such as being overweight, having a sedentary lifestyle, or having a family history of the disease.

Myth: Diabetes is not a serious condition.

This myth couldn't be further from the truth. Diabetes is a serious chronic condition that can lead to severe complications if left unmanaged. Uncontrolled blood sugar levels can damage vital organs, including the eyes, kidneys, nerves, and cardiovascular system. Proper management of diabetes through a balanced diet, regular exercise, and medication (if prescribed) is crucial to prevent or delay these complications and maintain overall health.

Myth: People with diabetes can't eat sweets or carbohydrates.

While it's true that individuals with diabetes need to be mindful of their carbohydrate intake, they do not have to completely eliminate sweets or carbohydrates from their diet. The key is moderation and portion control. With careful meal planning and the guidance of a healthcare professional or registered dietitian, people with diabetes can enjoy a wide variety of foods, including those containing carbohydrates and natural sugars, while maintaining healthy blood sugar levels.

Myth: Diabetes is contagious.

Diabetes is not a contagious disease and cannot be transmitted from one person to another. Type 1 diabetes is an autoimmune condition where the body's immune system attacks and destroys the insulin-producing cells in the pancreas. Type 2 diabetes is a metabolic disorder influenced by factors such as genetics, obesity, and lifestyle choices.

Neither type of diabetes is caused by a virus or bacteria that can be spread from person to person.

Myth: Insulin cures diabetes.

While insulin is a life-saving medication for individuals with type 1 diabetes and some cases of type 2 diabetes, it is not a cure. Insulin is a hormone that helps regulate blood sugar levels, but it does not address the underlying causes of the disease. Individuals with diabetes who take insulin still need to follow a healthy lifestyle, including a balanced diet and regular physical activity, to manage their condition effectively.

By dispelling these myths and misconceptions, individuals with diabetes and their loved ones can better understand the condition and make informed decisions about their health.

Jarrell Knox

CHAPTER 2

BUILDING A DIABETIC-FRIENDLY KITCHEN

Essential Kitchen Tools and Equipment

Navigating the kitchen as a beginner with diabetes can seem daunting, but having the right tools and equipment can make meal preparation a breeze. These essential items will not only simplify your cooking tasks but also aid in portion control and healthy eating habits.

A good set of measuring cups and spoons is crucial for accurately portioning ingredients, ensuring proper nutrient intake, and maintaining blood sugar levels. Opt for durable, easy-to-read sets that include both dry and liquid measures.

Investing in a quality non-stick cookware set can make cooking diabetic-friendly meals a pleasure. Look for pots and pans made of safe, non-reactive materials that distribute heat evenly and require minimal added oils or fats.

A sharp chef's knife and a cutting board are indispensable for slicing, dicing, and mincing fresh produce, lean proteins, and other wholesome ingredients. A sturdy wooden or plastic board is recommended for its durability and easy cleaning.

A food scale can be a game-changer for precise portion control, especially when it comes to measuring out complex carbohydrates like grains, pasta, and baked goods. Digital scales with a tare function make the process even simpler.

For those who enjoy meal prepping or batch cooking, airtight food storage containers in various sizes are a must-have. Glass or BPA-free plastic options are ideal for storing leftovers and prepped ingredients safely.

A high-powered blender or food processor can be a versatile ally in creating smooth, nutrient-dense smoothies, dips, sauces, and even homemade nut butter. Look for models with multiple speed settings and durable blades.

A slow cooker or Instant Pot can be a lifesaver for busy weeknights, allowing you to prepare wholesome, diabetic-friendly meals with minimal effort. These appliances are perfect for one-pot dishes, soups, stews, and even meal prepping.

For perfectly cooked proteins and veggies, a grill pan or indoor grill can be a valuable addition to your kitchen arsenal. These tools allow you to achieve those coveted grill marks and smoky flavors without added oils or fats.

A spiralizer is a fun tool that can transform fresh vegetables into noodle-like strands, providing a low-carb alternative to traditional pasta. It's an excellent way to increase your vegetable intake while satisfying those cravings for pasta dishes.

Finally, a good set of baking essentials, including silicone mats, whisks, and a quality oven thermometer, can ensure your diabetic-friendly baked goods turn out perfectly every time.

Stocking a Diabetic-Friendly Pantry

When it comes to managing diabetes, having a well-stocked pantry is half the battle. By filling your shelves with the right ingredients, you'll be empowered to create flavorful, nutrient-dense meals that support your health and wellness goals. Let's explore the essential elements of a diabetic-friendly pantry.

- **Whole Grains:** Opt for nutrient-rich whole grains over their refined counterparts. Stock up on brown rice, quinoa, whole-wheat pasta, and high-fiber cereals. These complex carbohydrates provide a steady stream of energy and help regulate blood sugar levels.

- **Legumes:** Lentils, chickpeas, black beans, and kidney beans are fantastic sources of fiber, protein, and essential nutrients. They're versatile ingredients that can be incorporated into soups, salads, and main dishes, adding depth and texture to your meals.

- **Nuts and Seeds:** Keep an assortment of unsalted nuts and seeds on hand for a satisfying crunch and a boost of healthy fats. Almonds, walnuts, chia seeds, and flaxseeds are excellent options that can be sprinkled over yogurt, oatmeal, or salads.

- **Low-Sodium Broths and Canned Goods:** Stock up on low-sodium vegetable and chicken broths for soups and stews. Canned tomatoes, artichokes, and olives can add flavor and variety to your dishes without excessive sodium or added sugars.

- **Spices and Herbs:** A well-curated spice rack is a diabetic's best friend. Dried herbs like basil, oregano, and rosemary, as well as spices like cumin, paprika, and turmeric, can infuse your meals with robust flavors, reducing the need for salt or sugar.

- **Low-Glycemic Sweeteners:** While it's best to limit added sugars, having a few low-glycemic sweeteners on hand can satisfy your sweet tooth in moderation. Options like stevia, monk fruit, or erythritol can be used in baking or to sweeten beverages without spiking your blood sugar levels.

- **Heart-Healthy Oils:** Opt for heart-healthy oils like extra-virgin olive oil, avocado oil, or coconut oil for cooking and dressing salads. These oils provide essential fatty acids and can help promote satiety, making it easier to manage portions.

- **Low-Sugar Condiments:** Choose low-sugar condiments like mustard, vinegar, and hot sauces to add flavor without excessive carbohydrates or added sugars.

When stocking your pantry, remember to read nutrition labels carefully and prioritize foods with high fiber and protein content, as well as those low in added sugars and sodium. With a well-curated pantry, you'll have the building blocks for delicious, diabetes-friendly meals at your fingertips.

Reading and Understanding Nutrition Labels

Navigating the world of nutrition labels can be a daunting task, especially for those newly diagnosed with diabetes. However, understanding how to read and interpret these labels is crucial for making informed decisions about the foods you consume.

Let's start with the basics: the Nutrition Facts panel. This standardized label provides a wealth of information about the nutrient content of a particular food item. At the top, you'll find the serving size and the number of servings per container or package. It's important to note that the values listed on the label are based on a single serving, so be mindful of your portion sizes.

Next, you'll see the calorie count, followed by the amounts of various macronutrients: total fat, saturated fat, trans fat, cholesterol, sodium, total carbohydrates, dietary fiber, total sugars, and protein. For those with diabetes, paying close attention to the total carbohydrate and total sugar content is particularly important, as these directly impact blood glucose levels.

When it comes to carbohydrates, remember that not all carbs are created equal. Look for foods that are high in fiber and low in added sugars. Fiber can help slow the absorption of glucose into the bloodstream, while excessive added sugars can lead to spikes in blood sugar levels.

Speaking of added sugars, this section on the label provides valuable insight into the amount of sugar that has been added during processing or manufacturing. It's generally recommended to limit your intake of added sugars, as they offer little to no nutritional value.

Moving on, you'll find the percent daily values (%DV) for various nutrients. These values are based on a 2,000-calorie diet and provide a reference point for determining if a food item is high or low in a particular nutrient. For example, a food item with 20% DV or more of a nutrient is considered high, while 5% DV or less is considered low.

When it comes to managing diabetes, paying attention to the %DV for carbohydrates, fiber, and sodium can be particularly helpful. Aim for foods that are low in carbohydrates and high in fiber, while also keeping an eye on your sodium intake, as excessive sodium can contribute to other health issues.

Don't forget to scan the ingredient list as well. Ingredients are listed in descending order by weight, so the first few items on the list make up the bulk of the product. Be wary of ingredients like added sugars (listed under different names like sucrose, high-fructose corn syrup, and maltose) and refined carbohydrates like white flour.

Meal Planning and Preparation Tips

Effective meal planning and preparation are crucial components of a diabetes-friendly lifestyle. By taking control of your kitchen and embracing mindful practices, you can ensure that your meals are not only delicious but also tailored to your specific dietary needs.

Establishing a Routine:

Creating a consistent routine can simplify the meal planning process and reduce the likelihood of impulsive, unhealthy choices. Consider the following:

- Schedule regular grocery shopping trips to ensure you have fresh, nutritious ingredients on hand.

- Dedicate a specific day or evening to meal-prepping for the week ahead.
- Involve family members or housemates in the process, making it a collaborative effort.

Meal Planning Essentials:

Thoughtful meal planning can help you maintain a balanced diet, manage portion sizes, and ensure variety in your meals. Keep these tips in mind:

- Plan meals and snacks in advance, considering your dietary requirements and preferences.
- Incorporate a variety of nutrient-dense foods, including lean proteins, whole grains, fruits, and vegetables.
- Experiment with new recipes and flavor combinations to keep your meals interesting and enjoyable.
- Consider batch cooking and freezing portions for quick, convenient meals on busy days.

Grocery Shopping Strategies:

Smart grocery shopping habits can make a significant difference in your ability to stick to a diabetic-friendly diet. Follow these guidelines:

- Create a detailed grocery list based on your meal plan to avoid impulse purchases.
- Read nutrition labels carefully, paying attention to carbohydrate content, fiber, and added sugars.
- Opt for whole, unprocessed foods whenever possible, as they are typically lower in added sugars and unhealthy fats.
- Stock up on non-perishable items like canned or frozen vegetables, beans, and whole grains for quick meal additions.

Kitchen Organization and Preparation:

An organized kitchen and streamlined preparation process can save time and reduce stress. Consider these tips:

- Keep frequently used diabetic-friendly ingredients and tools within easy reach.
- Invest in quality kitchen tools and equipment that make food preparation more efficient.
- Prep ingredients in advance, such as chopping vegetables or marinating proteins, to save time during meal assembly.
- Utilize kitchen gadgets like slow cookers, pressure cookers, or air fryers for hands-off cooking convenience.

Portion Control and Mindful Eating:

Maintaining portion control and practicing mindful eating are essential for effective diabetes management. Here are some helpful strategies:

- Use smaller plates and bowls to control portion sizes visually.
- Measure and weigh ingredients during preparation to ensure accurate serving sizes.
- Practice mindful eating by slowing down, savoring each bite, and paying attention to hunger and fullness cues.
- Avoid distractions like television or electronics during mealtimes to prevent mindless overeating.

By incorporating these meal planning and preparation tips into your routine, you'll be well on your way to creating a sustainable, diabetes-friendly lifestyle.

Jarrell Knox

CHAPTER 3

BREAKFAST DELIGHTS

Overnight Oats and Chia Puddings

Overnight oats and chia puddings are two delightful breakfast options that offer a convenient, nutrient-dense, and diabetic-friendly start to your day. These make-ahead meals not only save you time in the morning but also provide a satisfying and flavorful way to incorporate whole grains, fiber, and protein into your diet.

Overnight Oats:

Overnight oats are a versatile and customizable breakfast treat that can be tailored to suit your taste preferences. Simply combine rolled oats, milk (dairy or plant-based), and your desired mix-ins in a jar or bowl, and let it chill in the refrigerator overnight. The oats will absorb the liquid, resulting in a creamy, pudding-like texture.

To prepare overnight oats, you'll need:

- Rolled oats
- Milk (dairy or plant-based, such as almond, oat, or soy milk)
- Mix-ins (fresh or frozen berries, nut butter, seeds, cinnamon, vanilla extract, etc.)

Experiment with different flavor combinations by adding ingredients like:

- Peanut butter and banana
- Mixed berries and almonds
- Mango and coconut
- Cinnamon and apples

Chia Puddings:

Chia puddings are another make-ahead breakfast option that packs a nutritional punch. Chia seeds, when combined with milk or plant-based milk, form a thick, pudding-like consistency as they absorb the liquid. This makes for a filling and fiber-rich breakfast option.

To prepare chia pudding, you'll need:

- Chia seeds
- Milk (dairy or plant-based)
- Sweetener (optional: honey, maple syrup, or a sugar substitute)
- Flavor additions (vanilla extract, cocoa powder, fresh fruit, etc.)

Here are a few delicious chia pudding variations to try:

- Chocolate chia pudding (with cocoa powder and a touch of maple syrup)
- Vanilla and mixed-berry chia pudding
- Coconut chia pudding (with coconut milk and shredded coconut)
- Lime and mango chia pudding

Both overnight oats and chia puddings can be easily customized to suit your taste preferences and dietary needs. They are an excellent source of fiber, protein, and various nutrients, making them a satisfying and diabetes-friendly breakfast option.

Additionally, these make-ahead meals are incredibly convenient for busy mornings. Simply prepare them the night before, and they'll be ready for you to grab and enjoy on the go. Experiment with different flavor combinations and mix-ins to keep your breakfasts exciting and flavorful.

Savory Breakfast Skillets

Kick-start your day with a burst of flavors and nutrients by indulging in a delectable savory breakfast skillet. These hearty, all-in-one dishes are a perfect way to combine lean proteins, vibrant veggies, and wholesome grains into a satisfying and diabetes-friendly meal. Whether you're a fan of classic breakfast staples or eager to explore new culinary horizons, these skillet creations are sure to tantalize your taste buds while supporting your dietary needs.

For those who crave a taste of the Southwest, a Mexican-inspired skillet is a must-try. Start with a base of scrambled eggs or tofu, then layer in sautéed bell peppers, onions, and zesty spices like cumin and chili powder. Top it off with diced tomatoes, avocado slices, and a sprinkle of crumbled queso fresco for a burst of flavor and texture.

Transport your taste buds to the Mediterranean with a skillet brimming with roasted vegetables, crumbled feta, and a drizzle of tangy tzatziki sauce. Sautéed spinach, tomatoes, and zucchini provide a vibrant backdrop, while a sprinkle of oregano and a squeeze of lemon juice add an extra zing of flavor.

For a heartier option, a breakfast skillet loaded with diced potatoes, bell peppers, onions, and lean turkey sausage or bacon crumbles is sure to satisfy. Finish it off with a sprinkle of shredded cheddar cheese and a dollop of salsa or guacamole for a crowd-pleasing twist.

Embrace the flavors of the Middle East with a skillet filled with sautéed mushrooms, spinach, and crumbled feta or tofu. Seasoned with warm spices like cumin, cinnamon, and paprika, this dish is a delightful departure from traditional breakfast fare.

For a taste of the Mediterranean, a skillet brimming with roasted cherry tomatoes, sautéed zucchini, and crumbled feta or goat cheese is a must-try. Finish it off with a drizzle of balsamic glaze and a sprinkle of fresh basil for a burst of flavor.

Vegetarians and vegans can rejoice with a skillet filled with sautéed kale, roasted sweet potatoes, and black beans or lentils. Seasoned with smoked paprika and a touch of maple syrup, this dish is both nutritious and delightfully satisfying.

Diabetes-Friendly Pancakes and Waffles

Indulging in a stack of fluffy pancakes or crisp waffles is a breakfast tradition that many think they must forgo after a diabetes diagnosis. However, with a few simple adjustments and clever substitutions, you can savor these beloved morning treats without spiking your blood sugar levels. Prepare to elevate your breakfast game with delectable, diabetes-friendly pancakes and waffles that are sure to become new family favorites.

- Embrace Whole Grains: Ditch the refined white flour and embrace the nourishing goodness of whole grains. Opt for whole-wheat flour, oat flour, or a blend of both for a fiber-rich base that will keep you feeling satisfied and energized throughout the morning. Alternatively, try experimenting with nutrient-dense alternatives like almond flour, coconut flour, or buckwheat flour for a unique twist on traditional pancakes and waffles.

- Incorporate Nutrient-Boosters: Amp up the nutritional value of your pancakes and waffles by incorporating ingredients like mashed ripe bananas, pureed pumpkin, or grated zucchini. These additions not only add natural sweetness and moisture but also contribute valuable vitamins, minerals, and fiber to your breakfast.

- Sweeten with Caution: While a touch of sweetness can enhance the flavor of your pancakes and waffles, it's crucial to be mindful of the type and amount of sweetener you use. Opt for natural, low-glycemic options like pure maple syrup, monk fruit sweetener, or a moderate amount of mashed, ripe bananas. Avoid processed sugars and artificial sweeteners, which can cause blood sugar spikes and crashes.

- Experiment with Protein-Rich Toppings: Transform your pancakes and waffles into a well-rounded meal by topping them with protein-rich ingredients. Consider options like Greek yogurt, nut butters, or a sprinkle of nuts and seeds. These toppings not only add flavor and texture but also contribute to a sustained feeling of fullness, helping to manage cravings and prevent overeating later in the day.

- Get Creative with Flavors: Don't be afraid to think outside the box when it comes to flavoring your diabetes-friendly pancakes and waffles. Incorporate warm spices like cinnamon, nutmeg, or ginger for a cozy, autumnal twist. Or, experiment with fresh or frozen berries, citrus zest, or a hint of vanilla extract for a burst of refreshing flavors.

- Batch Cooking and Meal Prep: Pancakes and waffles can be easily made in advance and reheated for a convenient, grab-and-go breakfast option. Consider doubling or tripling your recipe and freezing the extras for busy mornings when time is limited. Simply pop them in the toaster or microwave for a quick and satisfying meal.

Smoothies and Juices

Smoothies and juices can be delicious and nutritious additions to a diabetic-friendly diet, providing a convenient way to incorporate a variety of fruits, vegetables, and other beneficial ingredients. However, it's essential to approach them with caution, as some options can be high in sugars and carbohydrates, potentially spiking blood glucose levels.

When it comes to smoothies, the key is to strike a balance between nutrient-dense ingredients and portion control. Start by choosing a protein-rich base, such as Greek yogurt, plant-based milk alternatives, or a scoop of protein powder. These will help slow down the absorption of sugars and provide a satisfying, filling texture.

Next, incorporate fibrous fruits and vegetables like berries, spinach, kale, avocado, and chia seeds. These nutrient-packed ingredients not only add valuable vitamins, minerals, and antioxidants but also contribute to a feeling of fullness and can help regulate blood sugar levels.

If you're looking to add sweetness, consider using small amounts of natural sweeteners like dates, honey, or maple syrup in moderation. These alternatives can provide a touch of sweetness without the drastic spike in blood sugar levels that refined sugars can cause.

Another option is to experiment with unsweetened nut butters, cocoa powder, or spices like cinnamon, which can add depth of flavor without contributing significant amounts of sugar or carbohydrates.

When it comes to juices, it's essential to understand that most store-bought varieties are high in concentrated sugars and lack the fiber found in whole fruits and vegetables. This can lead to rapid spikes in blood glucose levels, which can be detrimental for those with diabetes.

If you choose to enjoy juices, opt for those made from low-glycemic fruits like berries, citrus fruits, or green leafy vegetables. These options are generally lower in natural sugars and can provide a nutritious boost. Alternatively, consider diluting fruit juices with water or sparkling water to reduce the sugar concentration.

For a refreshing and diabetes-friendly option, try infusing water with sliced fruits, vegetables, and herbs. This can provide a subtle hint of flavor without the added sugars found in many juices.

When preparing smoothies or juices at home, it's crucial to measure and track the ingredients carefully. Invest in a quality blender or juicer that can efficiently extract nutrients from whole fruits and vegetables, ensuring you're consuming the fiber-rich pulp and skins.

Remember, while smoothies and juices can be a convenient way to incorporate more fruits and vegetables into your diet, they should be consumed in moderation and as part of a balanced meal plan. Consult with your healthcare provider or a registered dietitian to determine the appropriate portion sizes and frequency that align with your individual dietary needs and glucose management goals.

By following these guidelines and exercising portion control, you can enjoy the refreshing and nutritious benefits of smoothies and juices while effectively managing your diabetes.

Egg-cellent Dishes

Eggs are a true powerhouse when it comes to diabetes-friendly cuisine. Not only are they incredibly versatile and easy to prepare, but they also boast an impressive nutritional profile that makes them an excellent choice for those managing their blood sugar levels.

Nutritional Highlights:

Before diving into the recipes, let's appreciate the remarkable nutritional value of eggs. These incredible edibles are:

- Rich in high-quality protein, it is essential for building and repairing tissues and promoting satiety.

- A good source of vitamins and minerals, including vitamins A, D, E, B12, and choline, as well as iron, zinc, and selenium,.

- They are low in carbohydrates, making them a fantastic option for those following a diabetic-friendly diet.

- Packed with lutein and zeaxanthin, potent antioxidants that support eye health,.

Egg-ceptional breakfast options:

Start your day off right with these delightful and diabetes-friendly egg dishes that are sure to keep you feeling energized and satisfied:

- Fluffy Veggie Omelets: Fill your omelets with an array of colorful vegetables like spinach, bell peppers, and mushrooms for a nutrient-dense and fiber-rich breakfast.

- Baked Egg Cups: Whip up a batch of these portable and portion-controlled egg cups filled with your favorite ingredients, such as ham, cheese, and tomatoes.

- Egg Muffin Sandwiches: Craft homemade versions of classic breakfast sandwiches using whole-wheat English muffins, egg patties, and lean protein like turkey or avocado.

- Frittatas and Quiches: These versatile egg dishes can be loaded with an endless combination of vegetables, lean meats, and herbs for a satisfying and diabetes-friendly meal.

Beyond Breakfast:

Eggs aren't just for breakfast! Their versatility allows you to incorporate them into various dishes throughout the day. Consider these tempting options:

- Egg Salad Sandwiches: Elevate the classic egg salad by using Greek yogurt instead of mayonnaise and serving it on whole-grain bread or lettuce wraps.

- Vegetable Fritters: Mix shredded veggies like zucchini, carrots, or sweet potatoes with eggs and spices for crispy, nutrient-packed fritters.

- Breakfast Burritos: Wrap scrambled eggs, sautéed veggies, and lean protein like turkey or tofu in a whole-wheat tortilla for a portable and diabetes-friendly meal.

- Deviled Eggs: Transform hard-boiled eggs into delightful appetizers or snacks by mixing the yolks with Greek yogurt, Dijon mustard, and your favorite herbs and spices.

Tips and Tricks:

To ensure your egg dishes are as delicious and diabetes-friendly as possible, keep these tips in mind:

- Opt for cooking methods like scrambling, poaching, or baking to minimize the need for added fats.

- Incorporate fresh herbs, spices, and aromatics like garlic and onions to boost flavor without relying on excess salt or sugar.

- Pair your egg dishes with whole-grain toast, fresh fruits, or a side of roasted vegetables for a well-rounded and nutritious meal.

- Experiment with egg substitutes like egg whites or plant-based alternatives for added variety and to reduce cholesterol intake.

With their incredible versatility, nutritional punch, and endless recipe possibilities, eggs are a true staple in any diabetes-friendly kitchen. Embrace these egg-cellent dishes and let your culinary creativity soar, all while nourishing your body and managing your blood sugar levels with ease.

Jarrell Knox

CHAPTER 4

NUTRITIOUS LUNCHES AND LIGHT MEALS

Wholesome Salads and Grain Bowls

Salads and grain bowls are versatile, nutrient-packed options that can be tailored to suit your diabetic-friendly dietary needs. These dishes offer a perfect canvas for combining a variety of fresh vegetables, lean proteins, and whole grains, creating a balanced and satisfying meal. By embracing these wholesome choices, you can enjoy flavorful and diverse culinary adventures while managing your blood sugar levels effectively.

Let's begin with salads, a timeless favorite that can be transformed into a complete meal with the right ingredients. Start with a base of leafy greens, such as spinach, arugula, or mixed greens, and build upon it with a colorful array of vegetables like tomatoes, cucumbers, bell peppers, and carrots. To add a touch of heartiness, consider incorporating roasted or grilled vegetables, such as zucchini, eggplant, or Brussels sprouts.

For a protein boost, top your salad with lean options like grilled chicken, salmon, or plant-based sources like lentils, chickpeas, or tofu. Sprinkle in some nuts or seeds for a crunchy texture and an extra dose of healthy fats. Dress your salad with a homemade vinaigrette made from olive oil, vinegar, and your favorite herbs and spices for a burst of flavor without compromising your blood sugar levels.

Grain bowls offer another delightful way to combine various nutrient-dense ingredients into a single, satisfying dish. Start by selecting a whole grain base, such as quinoa, brown rice, farro, or bulgur. These complex carbohydrates provide lasting energy and fiber, making them an excellent choice for managing blood sugar levels.

Next, add a variety of roasted or sautéed vegetables, such as sweet potatoes, bell peppers, onions, and broccoli. For a protein component, consider grilled chicken, turkey, or plant-based options like tofu or tempeh. Top your grain bowl with a sprinkle of nuts or seeds for added crunch and healthy fats.

To enhance the flavor profile, consider incorporating fresh herbs like cilantro, basil, or parsley, and dress your bowl with a flavorful vinaigrette or a drizzle of tahini or hummus. You can also experiment with different ethnic flavors by incorporating spices like cumin, paprika, or ginger, or adding a dollop of salsa or tzatziki sauce.

Both salads and grain bowls can be easily customized to suit your individual preferences and dietary needs. They are highly versatile, allowing you to incorporate a wide variety of nutritious ingredients while ensuring a balanced intake of carbohydrates, proteins, and healthy fats.

Embrace the art of building your own wholesome salads and grain bowls, and you'll discover a world of delicious and diabetes-friendly options that will keep your taste buds satisfied and your blood sugar levels in check.

Soups and Stews for All Seasons

When it comes to diabetic-friendly meals, few dishes can match the versatility and nourishing qualities of soups and stews. These one-pot wonders not only pack a punch of flavor but also offer a canvas for incorporating an array of wholesome ingredients tailored to your dietary needs. From hearty, stick-to-your-ribs creations to light and refreshing options, there's a soup or stew to suit every palate and season.

As the chill of autumn settles in, cozy up with a steaming bowl of butternut squash soup. Roast the squash to bring out its natural sweetness, then blend it with vegetable or chicken broth, a splash of unsweetened almond milk, and warm spices like cinnamon and nutmeg. Top it with a sprinkle of toasted pumpkin seeds for added crunch and nutrition.

When the winter winds howl, nothing beats a robust beef and barley stew. Start by searing lean beef cubes in a hot pot, then add diced vegetables like carrots, celery, and onions. Simmer the mixture with low-sodium beef broth, pearl barley, and a touch of red wine or tomato paste for depth of flavor. Thicken the stew with a sprinkle of whole-wheat flour or a cornstarch slurry for a velvety texture.

As spring blossoms, celebrate the season with a vibrant asparagus and lemon soup. Sauté fresh asparagus with garlic and shallots, then blend with low-sodium vegetable broth and a squeeze of lemon juice. Finish it off with a dollop of creamy Greek yogurt and a sprinkle of fresh dill for a bright and refreshing bowl.

When the summer sun beats down, cool off with a chilled gazpacho. Blend ripe tomatoes, cucumbers, bell peppers, red onion, garlic, and a splash of sherry vinegar for a burst of tangy flavors. Chill the mixture thoroughly and serve with a garnish of diced avocado, crumbled feta, and a drizzle of extra-virgin olive oil.

For a heartier option, a lentil and kale stew is a nutritional powerhouse. Sauté diced onions, carrots, and celery in a pot, then add rinsed lentils, vegetable broth, and a bundle of chopped kale. Season with smoked paprika, cumin, and a splash of apple cider vinegar for a depth of flavor that will warm you from the inside out.

Embrace the flavors of the Mediterranean with a fragrant chickpea and spinach stew. Sauté garlic and onions in olive oil, then add diced tomatoes, chickpeas, and a generous handful of fresh spinach. Season with cumin, coriander, and a squeeze of lemon juice for a bright and zesty twist.

Remember, soups and stews are endlessly customizable, allowing you to experiment with a variety of ingredients and flavors to suit your taste preferences and dietary needs. Whether you're seeking comfort in a bowl or a light and refreshing meal, these versatile dishes are sure to become staples in your diabetic-friendly repertoire.

Sandwiches and Wraps

Sandwiches and wraps are the epitome of convenience and versatility, making them ideal for a diabetes-friendly lifestyle. With a little creativity and the right ingredients, you can craft delectable handheld meals that are both nutritious and satisfying. Let's explore the art of crafting diabetes-friendly sandwiches and wraps that will tantalize your taste buds while keeping your blood sugar levels in check.

- **Embrace Whole Grains:** When it comes to bread or wraps, opt for whole-grain varieties that are rich in fiber and nutrients. Whole-wheat bread, multigrain wraps, or even lettuce leaves provide a sturdy base that will keep you feeling fuller for longer, thanks to their low glycemic index and high fiber content.

- **Prioritize Lean Proteins:** Lean proteins should be the star of your sandwich or wrap. Consider options like grilled or roasted chicken breast, tuna, turkey, or plant-based alternatives like tofu or tempeh. These protein-packed ingredients will help stabilize your blood sugar levels and provide lasting energy.

- **Load Up on Veggies:** Don't be shy about piling on the vegetables! Fresh greens like spinach, arugula, or romaine lettuce add crunch and valuable nutrients. Sliced tomatoes, cucumbers, bell peppers, and onions not only contribute flavor but also provide fiber, vitamins, and minerals.

- **Incorporate Healthy Fats:** Avocado, hummus, or a drizzle of olive oil can add creaminess and richness to your sandwiches and wraps while providing heart-healthy monounsaturated fats. These fats can help slow down the absorption of carbohydrates, resulting in a more gradual rise in blood sugar levels.

- **Experiment with Flavorful Condiments:** Say goodbye to sugary condiments and hello to flavorful alternatives like Dijon mustard, low-sodium salsa, or balsamic vinegar. These additions can elevate the taste of your sandwiches and wraps without spiking your blood sugar levels.

- **Get Creative with Fillings:** Don't be afraid to think outside the box when it comes to sandwich and wrap fillings. Consider options like roasted vegetables, grilled eggplant, or even homemade hummus or guacamole. These nutrient-dense fillings can add variety and excitement to your meals.

- **Portion Control:** While sandwiches and wraps can be a nutritious choice, it's important to be mindful of portion sizes. Stick to one or two modest-sized sandwiches or wraps per meal, and pair them with a side salad or a serving of fresh fruit for a well-rounded meal.

- **Meal Prep for Convenience:** Sandwiches and wraps are perfect for meal prepping. Assemble them in advance and store them in the refrigerator for a grab-and-go lunch or a quick dinner option. Just be mindful of ingredients that may not hold up well, like soggy lettuce or tomatoes, and consider packing them separately.

By embracing whole grains, lean proteins, and an abundance of vegetables, you can transform ordinary sandwiches and wraps into diabetes-friendly meals that are both delicious and nutritious. Remember, moderation and mindful ingredient choices are key to maintaining balanced blood sugar levels while enjoying these handheld delights.

Light Pasta and Rice Dishes

Pasta and rice dishes are often associated with heavy, carbohydrate-laden meals, but they can be excellent options for those managing diabetes when prepared thoughtfully. With a few simple adjustments, you can create light, flavorful pasta and rice dishes that are both satisfying and diabetes-friendly.

Start by choosing whole-grain varieties of pasta and rice. These options are higher in fiber, which can help slow down the absorption of glucose into the bloodstream, preventing rapid spikes in blood sugar levels. Brown rice, quinoa, whole-wheat pasta, and even alternative options like chickpea or lentil-based pastas can be excellent choices.

When preparing these dishes, portion control is key. While carbohydrates are an essential part of a balanced diet, it's important to be mindful of your serving sizes. A good rule of thumb is to aim for a portion of cooked pasta or rice that's about the size of your fist or a tennis ball.

To add bulk and nutrition to your pasta and rice dishes, incorporate an abundance of non-starchy vegetables. Sautéed or roasted vegetables like bell peppers, zucchini, eggplant, tomatoes, and spinach can add flavor, fiber, and valuable nutrients while keeping the overall carbohydrate content in check.

Lean proteins, such as grilled chicken, shrimp, or tofu, can also be a fantastic addition to these dishes. Protein not only helps to slow down the absorption of carbohydrates but also contributes to a feeling of fullness and satisfaction, making it easier to stick to appropriate portion sizes.

When it comes to sauces and dressings, opt for lighter options like tomato-based sauces, pesto, or vinaigrettes. These can provide flavor without adding excessive amounts of fat, calories, or hidden sugars that can be found in many cream-based sauces or dressings.

For an extra boost of flavor and nutrition, consider incorporating fresh herbs like basil, cilantro, or parsley. Not only do they add vibrant flavors, but they also provide antioxidants and nutrients that can benefit overall health.

If you're craving a creamy texture, try blending in a small amount of avocado or low-fat Greek yogurt to your pasta or rice dish. These ingredients can add richness and creaminess while providing healthy fats and protein.

Don't be afraid to experiment with different flavor combinations and cultural cuisines. Dishes like stir-fries with brown rice, Mediterranean-inspired grain bowls, or Mexican-style cauliflower rice can be both delicious and diabetes-friendly when prepared with mindful ingredient choices.

Jarrell Knox

CHAPTER 5

SATISFYING DINNERS

Lean Protein Mains

Protein is an essential macronutrient that plays a vital role in maintaining optimal health, especially for those living with diabetes. Lean protein sources not only help regulate blood sugar levels but also contribute to a feeling of satiety, making them an invaluable component of a well-balanced diabetic diet. In this comprehensive guide, we'll explore a mouthwatering array of lean protein main dishes that are sure to satisfy your cravings while keeping your diabetes management on track.

Poultry Perfection:

Chicken and turkey are excellent lean protein options that offer incredible versatility in the kitchen. From grilled and roasted preparations to flavorful stir-fries and casseroles, these feathered delights can be the star of countless diabetic-friendly meals. Consider these tantalizing options:

- Herb-Crusted Roasted Chicken: Infuse your roasted chicken with robust flavors by coating it with a blend of fresh herbs, garlic, and lemon zest.

- Turkey Meatballs in Marinara Sauce: Swap traditional beef for lean turkey and serve these flavorful meatballs over a bed of whole-wheat pasta or zucchini noodles.

- Grilled Chicken Skewers: Thread marinated chicken pieces onto skewers with colorful veggies for a vibrant and nutritious main dish.

Seafood Sensations:

Seafood is not only a delicious source of lean protein but also offers a wealth of heart-healthy omega-3 fatty acids, making it an excellent choice for those with diabetes. From succulent fish fillets to versatile shrimp and scallops, the ocean's bounty provides endless possibilities. Here are a few mouthwatering options:

- Baked Salmon with Lemon and Dill: This simple yet elegant dish showcases the delicate flavors of fresh salmon while keeping the preparation diabetes-friendly.

- Grilled Shrimp Skewers with Vegetable Kabobs: Combine juicy shrimp and an array of vibrant veggies for a flavor-packed and nutritious grilled delight.

- Seared Tuna Steaks with Avocado Salsa: Elevate your dinner with this restaurant-worthy dish featuring seared tuna steaks topped with a refreshing avocado salsa.

Lean Meat Marvels:

While red meat should be consumed in moderation, lean cuts can be an excellent source of protein for those with diabetes. When selecting lean meats, opt for cuts with minimal visible fat and prepare them using diabetes-friendly cooking methods. Here are some delicious options to consider:

- Grilled Flank Steak with Chimichurri Sauce: Tender and flavorful, this grilled flank steak is elevated by a vibrant and zesty chimichurri sauce.

- Pork Tenderloin with Apple Chutney: Lean pork tenderloin is a versatile canvas for a variety of flavors, like the sweet and tangy notes of this homemade apple chutney.

- Beef and Vegetable Kebabs: Thread lean beef cubes and an assortment of colorful vegetables onto skewers for a fun and diabetes-friendly grilling experience.

Plant-Powered Proteins:

For those seeking vegetarian or vegan options, plant-based proteins can be just as satisfying and nutritious. From hearty legumes to soy-based products and nutrient-dense grains, the possibilities are endless. Here are a few meatless main dish ideas to explore:

- Lentil and Quinoa Stuffed Peppers: Combine the protein-packed duo of lentils and quinoa with a medley of vegetables for a flavorful and filling plant-based dish.

- Tofu Stir-Fry with Mixed Veggies: Sautéed tofu absorbs the flavors of your favorite stir-fry sauce, making it a versatile and diabetes-friendly protein option.

- Tempeh Burgers with Avocado Spread: These hearty and satisfying burgers made from fermented soybeans are a delicious and diabetes-friendly alternative to traditional beef patties.

No matter your protein preference, the key to creating delicious and diabetes-friendly main dishes lies in embracing a variety of lean sources, experimenting with bold flavors, and incorporating an abundance of nutrient-dense vegetables. With a little creativity and these mouthwatering recipe ideas, you can confidently navigate your diabetic diet while indulging in satisfying and wholesome protein-packed meals.

Veggie-Packed Sides

Embracing a diabetes-friendly lifestyle doesn't mean sacrificing flavor or variety when it comes to mealtime. In fact, incorporating veggie-packed sides into your routine can be a delightful and nutritious way to enhance your culinary experiences. These vibrant and flavorful dishes not only complement your main courses but also provide essential nutrients, fiber, and a burst of natural sweetness to help manage blood sugar levels effectively.

Let's embark on a journey through a colorful array of veggie-packed sides that will tantalize your taste buds while nourishing your body.

- **Roasted Root Vegetables:** Roasting brings out the natural sweetness and caramelized flavors of root vegetables like carrots, beets, parsnips, and sweet potatoes. Toss them with olive oil, herbs, and spices, and roast until tender and slightly charred for a delightful depth of flavor. These nutrient-dense sides are packed with fiber, vitamins, and antioxidants, making them a perfect addition to any meal.

- **Sautéed Greens:** Leafy greens like spinach, kale, and Swiss chard are nutritional powerhouses that can be easily incorporated into your meals. Sauté them with garlic, onions, and a splash of vinegar or lemon juice for a vibrant and flavorful side dish. Greens are low in carbohydrates and rich in vitamins, minerals, and fiber, making them an excellent choice for blood sugar management.

- **Cauliflower Rice or Mash:** Cauliflower is a versatile vegetable that can be transformed into a low-carb alternative to rice or mashed potatoes. Grate or pulse cauliflower florets in a food processor for a rice-like texture, or steam and mash them with a touch of butter or olive oil for a creamy mash. Seasoned with herbs and spices, these dishes offer a satisfying and diabetes-friendly alternative to traditional carb-heavy sides.

- **Grilled or Roasted Vegetable Skewers:** Thread your favorite veggies, like bell peppers, zucchini, mushrooms, and cherry tomatoes, onto skewers and grill or roast them to perfection. The char and smoky flavors add depth and complexity to these vibrant sides. Serve them alongside your main course or enjoy them as a standalone dish for a burst of flavor and nutrients.

- **Zucchini Noodles or Squash Ribbons:** Swap out traditional pasta for zucchini noodles or ribbons of yellow squash for a low-carb and diabetes-friendly alternative. Spiralize or slice the vegetables into noodle-like shapes, then sauté or bake them with your favorite sauce or toppings. These veggie-based "noodles" are packed with fiber and low in carbohydrates, making them a satisfying and nutritious option.

One-Pot and Casserole Meals

Juggling the demands of managing diabetes while navigating the culinary world can be a daunting task, but one-pot and casserole meals are here to simplify your life. These effortless dishes not only streamline your cooking process but also offer a delightful blend of flavors and textures that cater to your dietary needs. From hearty casseroles brimming with wholesome ingredients to aromatic one-pot wonders, these recipes are sure to become staples in your diabetic-friendly repertoire.

Imagine sinking your fork into a piping hot lasagna, but without the guilt. Crafted with whole-wheat noodles, lean ground turkey or plant-based protein crumbles, and a rich tomato sauce infused with sautéed vegetables, this dish is a testament to the fact that comfort food can be both delicious and diabetes-friendly. Layer it with a creamy ricotta and spinach mixture for an extra burst of flavor and nutrients.

For a taste of the Mediterranean, a one-pot baked orzo with roasted vegetables and feta is a must-try. Toss together whole-wheat orzo, diced bell peppers, zucchini, cherry tomatoes, and crumbled feta, then drizzle with olive oil, lemon juice, and a sprinkle of dried oregano. Bake until the orzo is tender and the vegetables are caramelized, creating a symphony of flavors in every bite.

Craving something heartier? A beef and vegetable stew simmered in a rich, low-sodium broth is the perfect remedy. Start by searing lean beef cubes in a pot, then add diced carrots, celery, onions, and potatoes. Simmer the mixture with a splash of red wine or tomato paste for added depth, and finish it off with a sprinkle of fresh herbs for a burst of vibrant flavors.

For a twist on a classic, try a quinoa and black bean casserole. Layer fluffy quinoa with sautéed onions, bell peppers, and black beans, then top it with a zesty enchilada sauce and a sprinkle of shredded cheese. Bake until bubbly and golden, and serve with a dollop of Greek yogurt or avocado for a creamy contrast.

Embrace the flavors of the Southwest with a one-pot Mexican-inspired rice dish. Sauté diced onions, bell peppers, and garlic in a pot, then add rinsed brown rice, diced tomatoes, black beans, and a blend of cumin, chili powder, and smoked paprika. Simmer until the rice is tender and the flavors have melded, then garnish with fresh cilantro, diced avocado, and a squeeze of lime juice.

For a plant-based option, a lentil and vegetable bake is a nutritional powerhouse. Layer cooked lentils with sautéed mushrooms, spinach, and diced sweet potatoes, then top with a creamy cashew-based sauce infused with garlic and nutmeg. Bake until golden and bubbly, and serve with a side of roasted Brussels sprouts for a complete meal.

Ethnic and Cultural Cuisines

Navigating diabetes doesn't mean you have to sacrifice the rich flavors and traditions of ethnic and cultural cuisines. In fact, many of these culinary treasures offer a wealth of diabetes-friendly options that can add variety and excitement to your meal plan. With a few mindful adjustments and ingredient swaps, you can savor the authentic tastes of the world while maintaining healthy blood sugar levels.

- **Mediterranean Delights:** The Mediterranean diet is widely celebrated for its emphasis on fresh vegetables, whole grains, lean proteins, and heart-healthy fats. Embrace the vibrant flavors of Greek, Italian, and Middle Eastern cuisines by incorporating dishes like grilled fish with lemon and herbs, chickpea salads, and whole-wheat pitas filled with hummus and roasted veggies.

- **Indian Spice Odyssey:** Indian cuisine is a paradise for diabetics, with its abundance of aromatic spices and flavorful plant-based dishes. Lentil-based curries, such as dal or chana masala, are packed with fiber and protein, while vegetable curries like aloo gobi (cauliflower and potatoes) or saag paneer (spinach and cheese) offer a delicious balance of nutrients.

- **Mexican Fiesta:** Mexican cuisine is often associated with carb-heavy options like tortillas and rice, but with a few tweaks, you can enjoy its bold flavors while keeping your blood sugar in check. Opt for lettuce wraps or whole-grain tortillas, and fill them with lean proteins like grilled chicken or fish, alongside fresh salsa, avocado, and a sprinkle of low-fat cheese.

- **Asian Fusion:** Asian cuisines offer a wide range of diabetes-friendly options, from stir-fries packed with vegetables and lean proteins to sushi rolls wrapped in nutrient-dense nori seaweed. Experiment with cauliflower rice as a low-carb alternative to traditional white rice, and embrace the flavors of ginger, garlic, and soy sauce.

- **Caribbean Flair:** The vibrant flavors of Caribbean cuisine can be enjoyed while managing diabetes. Explore dishes like jerk chicken (seasoned with a blend of allspice, thyme, and scotch bonnet peppers), fish stews simmered in coconut milk, and hearty vegetable curries made with callaloo, a nutrient-dense leafy green.

When exploring ethnic and cultural cuisines, remember to pay attention to portion sizes, especially when it comes to carbohydrate-rich items like rice, naan, or tortillas. Balance your meals with plenty of non-starchy vegetables, lean proteins, and healthy fats to help regulate blood sugar levels.

Don't be afraid to experiment with new spices, herbs, and flavor combinations. These culinary treasures can transform even the simplest dishes into taste sensations that will excite your palate while supporting your diabetes management.

Embrace the diversity of ethnic and cultural cuisines, and you'll discover a world of flavors that not only nourish your body but also delight your senses, making your journey with diabetes a deliciously rewarding experience.

CHAPTER 6

GUILT-FREE SNACKS AND TREATS

Crunchy and Savory Snacks

Snacking can be a challenge when managing diabetes, but with a little creativity and mindfulness, you can enjoy crunchy and savory treats that satisfy your cravings without compromising your health.

One of the most versatile snack options is roasted vegetables. Toss sliced or cubed vegetables like Brussels sprouts, cauliflower, carrots, or beets with a light drizzle of olive oil, your favorite herbs and spices, and a pinch of salt. Roast them in the oven until crispy and golden brown, and you'll have a delightful, fiber-rich snack that's low in carbohydrates but packed with flavor.

For a protein-packed crunch, try making your own roasted chickpeas or edamame. Simply toss them with a bit of olive oil, salt, and your preferred seasonings, and roast until crispy. These legume-based snacks are not only satisfying but also provide a good source of plant-based protein and fiber, which can help regulate blood sugar levels.

If you're craving something savory and cheesy, baked cheese crisps or crackers made with almond or coconut flour can be an excellent option. These low-carb alternatives can be tailored to your taste preferences by incorporating different herbs, spices, or even a sprinkle of everything bagel seasoning.

For a twist on traditional chips, try making your own baked veggie chips using thinly sliced vegetables like zucchini, beets, or kale. Lightly coat them with olive oil or avocado oil and your favorite spices, and bake until crispy. These nutrient-dense chips not only provide a satisfying crunch but also offer a variety of vitamins, minerals, and antioxidants.

If you're a fan of nuts, you can create your own flavorful nut mixes by combining different varieties like almonds, pecans, walnuts, and pumpkin seeds. For an added kick, toss them with a blend of spices like chili powder, cumin, and paprika, or try a sweet and savory combination with a touch of cinnamon and a light drizzle of maple syrup.

Don't forget about the power of seeds! Sunflower, pumpkin, and chia seeds can make for a nutritious and crunchy snack when roasted or seasoned with herbs and spices. They're not only low in carbohydrates but also provide a good source of healthy fats, fiber, and various minerals.

For a savory and protein-rich option, consider hard-boiled eggs or slices of high-quality deli meat rolled up with cheese or avocado. These snacks offer a satisfying combination of protein, healthy fats, and minimal carbohydrates, helping to keep you feeling fuller for longer.

By incorporating these delicious and diabetes-friendly snack options into your routine, you'll not only satisfy your cravings but also provide your body with essential nutrients that support overall health and blood sugar management.

Fresh Fruit Desserts

When it comes to satisfying your sweet tooth while managing diabetes, fresh fruit desserts are a true gift from nature. Not only are they bursting with natural flavors and vibrant colors, but they also offer a treasure trove of essential nutrients, fiber, and antioxidants that can benefit your overall health.

The Beauty of Fresh Fruit:

Before we dive into the recipes, let's appreciate the incredible benefits that fresh fruits bring to the table:

- Naturally Low in Calories: Fresh fruits are generally low in calories, making them an ideal choice for those watching their weight and managing diabetes.

- Rich in Fiber: Many fruits are excellent sources of dietary fiber, which can help regulate blood sugar levels and promote feelings of fullness.

- Packed with Vitamins and Minerals: Fruits are nature's gift baskets, providing a wide range of essential vitamins, minerals, and antioxidants that support overall health.

- Hydrating and Refreshing: With their high water content, fresh fruits can help keep you hydrated and refreshed, especially during the warmer months.

Fruity Delights to Savor:

Now, let's dive into the sweet and tantalizing world of fresh fruit desserts that are sure to delight your senses:

- Grilled Peaches with Honey Yogurt Drizzle: Caramelized grilled peaches topped with a luscious honey-sweetened yogurt drizzle – a perfect balance of sweet and tangy flavors.

- Mixed Berry Parfaits: Layer creamy Greek yogurt with a medley of fresh berries and a sprinkle of crunchy granola for a delightful and diabetes-friendly parfait.

- Mango and Kiwi Fruit Salad: Celebrate the vibrant colors and flavors of tropical fruits by combining juicy mangoes, kiwis, and a zesty lime dressing.

- Baked Apples with Cinnamon and Walnuts: Enjoy the comforting aroma of baked apples infused with warming cinnamon and crunchy walnuts for a cozy and diabetes-friendly treat.

Creative Twists and Variations:

To keep your dessert game fresh and exciting, consider these creative twists and variations:

- Swap out traditional sugary toppings for a drizzle of honey, a sprinkle of cinnamon, or a dollop of unsweetened whipped cream.

- Experiment with different flavor combinations by pairing fruits with herbs like mint, basil, or rosemary for a unique and refreshing twist.

- Incorporate dairy-free alternatives like coconut yogurt or cashew-based cream for those following a vegan or dairy-free diet.

- Add a crunchy element by sprinkling chopped nuts, seeds, or a hint of granola over your fruit desserts for added texture and nutrition.

Tips for Perfectly Crafted Fruit Desserts:

To ensure your fresh fruit desserts are not only delicious but also diabetes-friendly, keep these tips in mind:

- Choose fruits that are in season for optimal flavor and nutrition.

- Portion control is key – even with fresh fruit desserts, moderation is essential for managing blood sugar levels.

- Consider pairing your fruit desserts with a source of lean protein, such as Greek yogurt or a handful of nuts, to help balance the glycemic impact.

- Opt for ripe, sweet fruits to minimize the need for added sweeteners, and experiment with natural sweeteners like honey or maple syrup if necessary.

With their vibrant colors, refreshing flavors, and wealth of health benefits, fresh fruit desserts are a true delight for anyone managing diabetes. Embrace the natural sweetness of nature's bounty and let your culinary creativity soar as you craft delectable and diabetes-friendly desserts that will leave you feeling satisfied and nourished from the inside out.

Diabetic-Friendly Baked Goods

Indulging in delectable baked goods while managing diabetes may seem like a challenge, but with a few smart substitutions and techniques, you can enjoy guilt-free treats without compromising your health. The key lies in embracing diabetes-friendly ingredients and portion control, allowing you to savor the flavors and textures you crave while keeping your blood sugar levels in check.

Let's dive into the world of diabetic-friendly baked goods and explore how you can satisfy your sweet tooth without sacrificing your well-being.

- Flourless Baked Treats: Ditch traditional wheat flour and opt for nutrient-dense alternatives like almond flour, coconut flour, or ground oats. These flours are low in carbohydrates and rich in fiber, protein, and healthy fats, making them excellent choices for diabetic-friendly baking. From fudgy brownies to moist cakes, the possibilities are endless when you embrace these versatile ingredients.

- Naturally Sweetened Delights: Bid farewell to refined sugars and embrace natural sweeteners like monk fruit, stevia, or erythritol. These low-calorie options provide a sweet taste without spiking your blood sugar levels. You can also experiment with fruit purees, such as mashed bananas or applesauce, to add natural sweetness and moisture to your baked goods.

- High-Fiber Treats: Incorporating fiber-rich ingredients like ground flaxseeds, chia seeds, or psyllium husk into your baked goods can help slow down the absorption of sugars, promoting a more gradual rise in blood sugar levels. These ingredients also contribute to a sense of fullness, preventing overeating and aiding in portion control.

- Protein-Packed Goodies: By incorporating protein-rich ingredients like Greek yogurt, cottage cheese, or nut butters into your baked goods, you can create treats that are not only delicious but also satisfying and nutrient-dense. The added protein helps stabilize blood sugar levels and keeps you feeling fuller for longer.

- Portion-Controlled Indulgences: While moderation is key, it's essential to remember that you can still enjoy your favorite treats in smaller portions. Consider baking your goodies in mini or individual serving sizes, allowing you to savor every bite without overindulging. This approach ensures that you can enjoy a sweet treat without compromising your diabetes management.

Embrace creative substitutions, experiment with new flavors, and celebrate the joy of baking with diabetes-friendly ingredients. From moist and fudgy brownies to tender and fluffy muffins, the possibilities are endless. With a little creativity and some smart swaps, you can indulge in delectable baked goods while maintaining a healthy and well-balanced lifestyle.

Frozen Treats and Smoothies

When the sweltering heat of summer hits or you're simply craving a refreshing indulgence, diabetic-friendly frozen treats and smoothies are the perfect solution. With a little creativity and the right ingredients, you can whip up delectable concoctions that not only satisfy your sweet tooth but also provide a burst of nutrients tailored to your dietary needs. Bid farewell to boring snacks and embrace the vibrant flavors and textures that these chilled delights have to offer.

For those who can't resist the allure of ice cream, homemade banana "nice" cream is a game-changer. Simply blend frozen, ripe bananas with a splash of unsweetened almond milk and a touch of vanilla extract until creamy and luscious. Customize your creation with a sprinkle of cinnamon, a drizzle of sugar-free chocolate or caramel sauce, or a handful of crushed nuts for an added crunch.

Embrace the tropical vibes with a mango and coconut frozen yogurt parfait. Layer Greek yogurt with diced mango, unsweetened shredded coconut, and a sprinkle of sliced almonds or granola for a burst of flavors and textures. Top it off with a drizzle of honey or a sugar-free syrup for an extra touch of sweetness.

Craving a refreshing smoothie? Blend together fresh spinach, frozen mango chunks, unsweetened almond milk, and a squeeze of lime juice for a tangy and nutrient-packed treat. Boost its creaminess with a dollop of Greek yogurt or a sprinkle of chia seeds for added protein and fiber.

Transport your taste buds to the tropics with a pineapple and coconut smoothie bowl. Blend frozen pineapple chunks, unsweetened coconut milk, and a touch of vanilla extract until thick and creamy. Pour the mixture into a bowl and top with fresh berries, sliced kiwi, unsweetened shredded coconut, and a sprinkle of granola for a vibrant and nutritious start to your day.

For a decadent yet diabetes-friendly treat, indulge in a chocolate avocado mousse. Blend together ripe avocado, unsweetened cocoa powder, a touch of maple syrup or stevia, and a splash of unsweetened almond milk until smooth and creamy. Chill the mixture and serve topped with fresh berries or a sprinkle of cinnamon for a rich and indulgent dessert.

Embrace the flavors of the Mediterranean with a refreshing watermelon and feta smoothie. Blend together cubed watermelon, crumbled feta cheese, fresh mint leaves, and a squeeze of lime juice for a tangy and revitalizing concoction that's perfect for beating the summer heat.

Experiment with different fruits, vegetables, dairy alternatives, and natural sweeteners to create unique and satisfying combinations that cater to your taste preferences and dietary needs. These chilled delights not only provide a refreshing respite from the heat but also offer a delightful way to nourish your body with a blend of essential nutrients.

Jarrell Knox

CHAPTER 7

BEVERAGES AND LIQUID REFRESHMENTS

Infused Waters and Teas

Staying hydrated is crucial for overall health, and it becomes even more essential when managing diabetes. While water is the obvious choice, infused waters and teas offer a delightful way to add flavor and variety to your daily hydration routine. By incorporating these refreshing beverages into your lifestyle, you can not only quench your thirst but also reap a host of additional benefits.

Infused Waters: A Flavorful Hydration Boost

Infused waters are a simple and budget-friendly way to add natural flavors to your water without the need for artificial sweeteners or sugary drinks. The possibilities are endless when it comes to creating your own custom blends.

- Fruit Infusions: Sliced citrus fruits like lemons, limes, and oranges are classic choices, but you can also experiment with berries, watermelon, pineapple, or even cucumber for a refreshing twist.

- Herbal Accents: Fresh herbs like mint, basil, rosemary, or lavender can add a delightful aroma and subtle flavor to your infused waters.

- Spice it Up: For a hint of warmth and depth, try infusing your water with slices of ginger, cinnamon sticks, or a dash of vanilla extract.

Teas: A Treasure Trove of Antioxidants

Teas have been revered for centuries for their health benefits, making them an excellent choice for individuals with diabetes. From classic black and green teas to herbal infusions, the options are vast and can cater to various taste preferences.

- Green Tea: Rich in antioxidants and proven to aid in regulating blood sugar levels, green tea is a diabetic-friendly powerhouse.

- Herbal Teas: Explore the world of herbal teas like chamomile, peppermint, and hibiscus, which can offer a myriad of benefits, from promoting relaxation to supporting digestion.

- Iced Tea: For a refreshing twist, brew a batch of unsweetened iced tea using black, green, or herbal varieties, and customize it with fresh fruit slices or a hint of lemon.

Brewing and Infusing Tips:

- Experiment with hot and cold infusions to find your preferred method.

- For hot infusions, let your fruits, herbs, or spices steep in boiling water for at least 10–15 minutes to extract maximum flavor.

- Cold infusions can be prepared by simply adding your desired ingredients to a pitcher of water and allowing it to infuse for several hours in the refrigerator.

- Adjust the steeping time and ingredient ratios to suit your taste preferences.

Hydration on the Go:

Infused waters and teas are perfect for staying hydrated throughout the day. Pack a reusable water bottle or travel mug filled with your favorite infusion to enjoy at work, during your commute, or while running errands.

By embracing the world of infused waters and teas, you'll not only satisfy your thirst but also add an exciting array of flavors and potential health benefits to your diabetes management routine. Experiment, get creative, and enjoy the refreshing journey of discovering your new favorite hydrating beverages.

Smoothies and Shakes

Smoothies and shakes can be delightfully refreshing and nutritious additions to a diabetes-friendly diet when prepared thoughtfully. However, it's essential to approach them with caution, as some options can be loaded with excess sugars, carbohydrates, and unhealthy fats, potentially spiking blood glucose levels.

Let's start with the foundational ingredients. Instead of relying solely on fruit juices or sweetened milk, opt for unsweetened plant-based milk alternatives like almond, coconut, or oat milk. These provide a creamy base without the added sugars found in many fruit juices or dairy milk. Greek yogurt or a scoop of protein powder can also be excellent additions, adding protein and thickness to your smoothie while helping to slow down the absorption of carbohydrates.

When it comes to fruits, select options that are lower in natural sugars and higher in fiber, such as berries (strawberries, raspberries, and blueberries), kiwi, and green apples. Incorporating leafy greens like spinach, kale, or Swiss chard can also boost the nutrient density of your smoothie while providing additional fiber to help regulate blood sugar levels.

For added creaminess and healthy fats, consider incorporating avocado, nut butters, or a moderate amount of seeds like chia, flax, or hemp. These ingredients not only provide a rich, satisfying texture but also contribute to a feeling of fullness, making it easier to stick to appropriate portion sizes.

If you're looking to add a touch of sweetness, try incorporating small amounts of natural sweeteners like dates, a drizzle of pure maple syrup, or a sprinkle of cinnamon. These alternatives can provide a subtle sweetness without the drastic spike in blood sugar levels that refined sugars can cause.

For an extra nutrient boost, consider adding a handful of nutrient-dense superfoods like acai, goji berries, spirulina, or matcha powder. These ingredients are packed with antioxidants, vitamins, and minerals that can support overall health and well-being.

When it comes to shakes, the key is to strike a balance between protein, healthy fats, and fiber-rich carbohydrates. Start with a base of unsweetened plant-based milk or Greek yogurt, and add a scoop of your favorite protein powder. Experiment with flavors like vanilla, chocolate, or even peanut butter powder for a delightful twist.

To ensure your shake is diabetes-friendly, incorporate ingredients like nut butters, avocado, or a small portion of whole grains like oats or quinoa. These ingredients can provide sustained energy and help regulate blood sugar levels while keeping you feeling satisfied for longer periods of time.

Don't be afraid to get creative with your smoothie and shake combinations. Try blending in fresh or frozen berries, a sprinkle of cinnamon or cocoa powder, or even a handful of fresh mint or basil for added flavor and nutrition.

Remember, portion control is crucial when it comes to smoothies and shakes. While they can be nutrient-dense, it's still essential to be mindful of the total carbohydrate and sugar content. Consider splitting a larger smoothie or shake into two servings, or enjoy a smaller portion as a snack alongside a balanced meal.

By incorporating these tips and strategies, you can create delightful, diabetes-friendly smoothies and shakes that not only satisfy your cravings but also provide a nutritious boost to your daily diet, supporting your journey toward better health and blood sugar management.

Mocktails and Cocktails

In the pursuit of a well-rounded, diabetes-friendly lifestyle, it's essential to embrace moments of indulgence andbration. While alcohol should be consumed in moderation, there's no reason to deprive yourself entirely, especially when you can craft delectable mocktails and cocktails that are both flavorful and mindful of your dietary needs.

The Art of Mocktails:

Mocktails are the perfect solution for those who prefer to abstain from alcohol or seek a non-alcoholic alternative. These sophisticated sippers offer a world of flavors without compromising on taste or presentation. Embrace these tantalizing options:

- Strawberry Basil Lemonade: Tart and refreshing, this vibrant mocktail combines the sweetness of fresh strawberries with the herbal notes of basil and the zing of lemon.

- Virgin Piña Colada: Transport yourself to a tropical paradise with this creamy, non-alcoholic twist on the classic piña colada, blended with pineapple, coconut, and a hint of lime.

- Ginger Mint Fizz: Invigorate your senses with this effervescent mocktail featuring zesty ginger, vibrant mint, and a bubbly splash of sparkling water or soda.

- Cucumber Melon Cooler: Beat the heat with this hydrating and refreshing combination of crisp cucumber, juicy melon, and a touch of lime for a subtle sweetness.

Crafting Diabetes-Friendly Cocktails:

For those who enjoy the occasional adult beverage, moderation and mindful choices are key. Here, we'll explore cocktail options that prioritize fresh, natural ingredients while minimizing added sugars and carbohydrates:

- Blueberry Gin Fizz: Elevate your cocktail game with this tangy and antioxidant-rich concoction featuring muddled blueberries, gin, and a splash of tonic water.

- Skinny Margarita: Indulge in the classic flavors of a margarita without the excessive sugar by blending tequila with freshly squeezed lime juice and a hint of agave nectar.

- Rosemary Vodka Sour: This herbaceous twist on the traditional sour cocktail combines vodka, fresh rosemary, lemon juice, and a touch of honey for a perfectly balanced sipper.

- Red Wine Spritzer: Enjoy the heart-healthy benefits of red wine in a refreshing and hydrating spritzer by combining it with sparkling water and a squeeze of fresh citrus.

Low-Carb Mixers and Alternatives:

To craft diabetes-friendly cocktails, it's essential to be mindful of the mixers and ingredients you choose. Here are some low-carb options to consider:

- Sparkling Waters and Club Sodas: These sugar-free carbonated beverages provide a refreshing base for cocktails without adding unnecessary carbohydrates.

- Fresh Citrus Juices: Lemon, lime, and grapefruit juices offer a vibrant and natural way to add tartness and flavor to your drinks.

- Unsweetened Teas and Herbal Infusions: From green tea to hibiscus, these flavorful brews can add depth and complexity to your mocktails and cocktails.

- Low-Calorie Sweeteners: If needed, opt for natural low-calorie sweeteners like monk fruit or stevia to add a touch of sweetness without spiking blood sugar levels.

Tips for Mindful Sipping:

Whether you're enjoying a refreshing mocktail or a carefully crafted cocktail, remember to savor each sip mindfully. Here are some tips to keep in mind:

- Pace yourself: Sip slowly and enjoy the flavors rather than drinking quickly. This will help you appreciate the beverage and stay in tune with your body's signals.

- Stay Hydrated: Alternate between alcoholic and non-alcoholic beverages and drink plenty of water to stay hydrated.

- Opt for Small Portions: When it comes to cocktails, consider ordering smaller portions or sharing with a friend to maintain moderation.

- Choose Quality Over Quantity: Savor a well-crafted, diabetes-friendly cocktail or mocktail rather than indulging in multiple sugary or carbohydrate-heavy beverages.

With a little creativity and a focus on fresh, natural ingredients, you can elevate your beverage game while maintaining a diabetes-friendly lifestyle. Raise a glass to these refreshing mocktails and cocktails, and toast to the joy of mindful indulgence and balanced living.

Jarrell Knox

CHAPTER 8

COOKING FOR SPECIAL OCCASIONS

Holiday Feasts and Gatherings

Navigating holiday feasts and gatherings can be a delicate balancing act when managing diabetes, but with the right strategies, you can savor the flavors and traditions without compromising your health. These joyous occasions are meant to be celebrated, and by embracing mindful choices and portion control, you can indulge in the festive spirit while maintaining stable blood sugar levels.

First and foremost, it's essential to approach holiday meals with a plan. Before attending a gathering, take a moment to familiarize yourself with the menu or ask the host about the dishes that will be served. This knowledge will empower you to make informed decisions and identify potential pitfalls or diabetes-friendly options.

When it comes to the main course, opt for lean protein sources like turkey, chicken, or fish, and pair them with a generous portion of non-starchy vegetables. These nutrient-dense choices will help you feel satiated while providing essential vitamins, minerals, and fiber to support healthy blood sugar levels.

If indulging in traditional holiday dishes like mashed potatoes or stuffing, practice portion control by limiting your servings to a reasonable amount. Consider using a smaller plate to encourage mindful eating and prevent overeating. Additionally, opt for whole-grain alternatives whenever possible, as they offer a slower release of sugars into the bloodstream.

Don't neglect the vibrant array of fresh fruits and vegetables often present during holiday gatherings. Load up your plate with colorful options like roasted Brussels sprouts, cranberry salad, or steamed green beans. These nutrient-packed choices will not only add flavor and variety to your meal but also provide valuable fiber and antioxidants to support overall health.

When it comes to desserts, moderation is key. Instead of depriving yourself entirely, savor a small portion of your favorite treat and balance it with a sensible meal or snack. Seek out diabetes-friendly dessert alternatives like fresh fruit with a dollop of Greek yogurt or a small slice of homemade pie made with natural sweeteners and whole-grain crusts.

Hydration is crucial during holiday festivities. Opt for water, unsweetened teas, or sparkling water infused with fresh fruit to quench your thirst and avoid sugary beverages that can spike blood sugar levels.

Remember, the true essence of holiday gatherings lies in the cherished connections and shared experiences, not just the food. Engage in lively conversations, participate in holiday traditions, and create lasting memories with your loved ones. By prioritizing mindful choices and embracing moderation, you can fully immerse yourself in the festivities while maintaining a healthy and balanced approach to diabetes management.

Lastly, be kind to yourself. If you overindulge or make a less-than-ideal choice, forgive yourself and simply get back on track with your next meal or snack. The journey to managing diabetes is an ongoing process, and every holiday gathering presents an opportunity to learn, grow, and celebrate life's precious moments.

Celebrations and Parties

Navigating celebrations and parties while managing diabetes can be a daunting task, but with a little preparation and a positive mindset, you can confidently indulge in the festivities without compromising your dietary needs. From decadent yet diabetic-friendly desserts to savory finger foods and cocktail offerings,.

When it comes to desserts, a showstopping flourless chocolate cake is sure to impress even the most discerning sweet tooth. Crafted with rich cocoa powder, almond flour, and a touch of sugar-free sweetener, this decadent treat is both diabetes-friendly and utterly indulgent. Top it with fresh berries and a dusting of powdered sugar substitute for a stunning presentation.

For a lighter option, try a refreshing lemon and blueberry trifle. Layer low-fat Greek yogurt with fresh blueberries, lemon zest, and crumbled whole-grain biscuits or angel food cake. Drizzle with a sugar-free lemon syrup for a burst of tangy flavor that's sure to delight your taste buds.

When it comes to savory offerings, mini quiches are a versatile and diabetes-friendly option. Whisk together eggs, low-fat milk or unsweetened almond milk, and your favorite fillings, like sautéed spinach, mushrooms, or diced ham. Pour the mixture into a muffin tin lined with whole-wheat phyllo dough or a homemade crust made with almond flour for bite-sized quiches that are perfect for sharing.

Embrace the flavors of the Mediterranean with a colorful vegetable and hummus platter. Arrange sliced bell peppers, cucumber, carrots, and cherry tomatoes around a bowl of creamy hummus made with chickpeas, tahini, garlic, and a squeeze of lemon juice. Serve with whole-grain pita chips or veggie sticks for a delightfully fresh and nutritious option.

For a touch of indulgence, offer a charcuterie board loaded with cured meats, low-fat cheeses, olives, nuts, and fresh or dried fruits. Pair it with whole-grain crackers or slices of crusty bread for a satisfying and diabetes-friendly grazing experience.

When it comes to cocktails, a refreshing cucumber and mint vodka spritzer is sure to be a crowd-pleaser. Muddle fresh cucumber slices and mint leaves in a glass, then top with vodka, lime juice, and a splash of seltzer water. Garnish with a cucumber ribbon and a sprig of mint for a vibrant and refreshing sip.

For a non-alcoholic option, try a fruity iced tea punch. Brew a batch of unsweetened black or herbal tea, then chill it and mix with fresh or frozen berries, sliced citrus fruits, and a touch of sugar-free sweetener or a sugar substitute. Top with sparkling water or club soda for a festive and diabetes-friendly beverage.

With these delectable and diabetes-friendly options, you can confidently savor the flavors and embrace the festivities without compromising your dietary needs or missing out on the joy of the occasion.

Game Day Bites

Game days are often associated with indulgent snacks and greasy treats, but for those managing diabetes, a little creativity can go a long way in crafting delicious, diabetes-friendly bites that satisfy cravings without derailing your health goals. Whether you're hosting a watch party or simply enjoying the game at home, these game-day bites will have you cheering for more.

Crunchy Veggie Platters:

Fresh vegetables are the ultimate game-day snack—packed with fiber, nutrients, and low in carbohydrates. Elevate your veggie tray by offering a variety of colorful options like carrot and cucumber sticks, bell pepper strips, cherry tomatoes, and radishes. Serve them with a tasty dip like tzatziki made with Greek yogurt, hummus, or a zesty guacamole for an extra burst of flavor.

Protein-Packed Skewers:

Skewers are not only fun to eat but also a great way to incorporate lean proteins into your game-day spread. Consider threading grilled chicken, shrimp, or tofu cubes with cherry tomatoes, bell peppers, and zucchini for a colorful and satisfying snack. Brush them with a flavorful marinade made with olive oil, herbs, and spices for an added kick.

Baked Crispy Chips:

Ditch the greasy potato chips and opt for homemade baked alternatives made from nutrient-dense ingredients. Thinly slice vegetables like kale, sweet potatoes, or beets, toss them with a light coating of olive oil and your favorite seasonings, and bake until crispy. Serve these crunchy treats with a tangy, yogurt-based dip for a satisfying crunch.

Stuffed Mushroom Caps:

Mushrooms are a low-carb, nutrient-rich canvas for creating flavorful game-day bites. Remove the stems from portobello or cremini mushroom caps and stuff them with a savory filling like a mixture of sautéed spinach, garlic, and feta cheese. Bake until tender, and enjoy these bite-sized morsels as a tasty and diabetes-friendly option.

Grilled Kabobs:

Fire up the grill and skewer chunks of your favorite lean meats, like chicken or beef, along with colorful vegetables like bell peppers, onions, and cherry tomatoes. Brush them with a flavorful marinade or rub, and grill until perfectly charred and tender. These protein-packed kabobs are a crowd-pleaser and can be easily customized to suit different dietary preferences.

No-Bake Energy Bites:

For a sweet treat without the sugar crash, whip up a batch of no-bake energy bites. Combine rolled oats, nut butter, honey or maple syrup, shredded coconut, and your favorite mix-ins like chopped nuts, seeds, or dried fruit. Roll the mixture into bite-sized balls and enjoy a satisfying, diabetes-friendly snack that's sure to fuel your game-day fun.

Jarrell Knox

CHAPTER 9

MEAL PLANNING AND LIFESTYLE TIPS

Creating a Balanced Plate

Crafting a balanced plate is an essential skill for anyone managing diabetes. By understanding the right proportions of different food groups and making mindful choices, you can enjoy delicious and satisfying meals while keeping your blood sugar levels in a healthy range.

The foundation of a balanced plate lies in the MyPlate method, which divides the plate into four sections: non-starchy vegetables, protein, grains, and fruits. This visual representation serves as a helpful guide for planning meals that include a variety of nutrient-dense foods.

Start by filling half of your plate with non-starchy vegetables, such as leafy greens, broccoli, cauliflower, carrots, or bell peppers. These nutrient-rich vegetables are low in carbohydrates and high in fiber, vitamins, and minerals, making them an excellent choice for maintaining stable blood sugar levels and promoting overall health.

For the protein portion, aim for lean sources like grilled or baked chicken, fish, tofu, or lean cuts of beef or pork. Protein helps to slow down the absorption of carbohydrates, keeping you feeling fuller for longer and preventing rapid spikes in blood sugar levels. Consider incorporating plant-based proteins like lentils, chickpeas, or edamame for added variety and fiber.

When it comes to grains, opt for whole-grain options like brown rice, quinoa, whole-wheat bread, or whole-grain pasta. These complex carbohydrates are higher in fiber and nutrients than their refined counterparts, helping to regulate blood sugar levels more effectively. Portion control is key, so aim for a serving size that fits comfortably in the grain section of your plate.

Lastly, incorporate a serving of fresh or frozen fruit, such as berries, citrus fruits, or a small apple or pear. Fruits provide natural sweetness, fiber, and a range of essential vitamins and minerals. However, be mindful of portion sizes, as some fruits can be higher in natural sugars.

To add flavor and variety to your balanced plate, consider incorporating healthy fats like avocado, nuts, or olive oil in moderation. These nutrient-dense fats can help enhance the absorption of certain vitamins and contribute to a feeling of satisfaction after your meal.

Remember, hydration is also an essential component of a balanced diet. Aim to drink plenty of water or unsweetened beverages throughout the day to support overall health and prevent dehydration.

Meal planning and preparation can also play a crucial role in creating balanced plates. Consider prepping ingredients in advance, such as chopping vegetables or marinating proteins, to make assembly quicker and easier during busy weeknights. Additionally, consider involving family members or friends in the meal planning process, as it can foster a sense of ownership and excitement around healthy eating habits.

By prioritizing a balanced plate with the right proportions of non-starchy vegetables, lean proteins, whole grains, and fruits, you'll be well on your way to managing your diabetes effectively while enjoying delicious and nourishing meals that support your overall health and well-being.

Portion Control Strategies

In the journey towards better health and effective diabetes management, portion control plays a crucial role. Striking the right balance between enjoying your favorite foods and maintaining stable blood sugar levels can be a game-changer. This comprehensive guide will equip you with practical strategies and techniques to help you navigate portion sizes with confidence, ensuring that every bite is both satisfying and supportive of your dietary needs.

Understanding Portion Sizes:

Before delving into strategies, let's demystify portion sizes and their importance in diabetes management.

- Portion sizes refer to the recommended amounts of food to consume in one sitting, based on factors such as calorie content, nutrient density, and individual dietary requirements.

- Portion control is essential for regulating blood sugar levels, as consuming excessive portions can lead to spikes in blood glucose and potential complications.

- Maintaining proper portion sizes can also aid in weight management, a crucial factor in reducing the risk of diabetes-related complications.

Visual Cues and Measurement Tools:

One of the most effective ways to grasp portion sizes is through visual cues and measurement tools. Here are some helpful techniques:

- • Use Your Hand: Utilize your hand as a handy portion guide. For example, a closed fist represents one portion of carbohydrates, while the palm of your hand approximates the size of a protein portion.

- Invest in Portion Control Plates: Consider purchasing plates or bowls designed with portion-specific compartments, guiding you on how much to serve for each food group.

- Measure with Household Items: Get creative with common household items like cups, spoons, or even a deck of cards to estimate portion sizes visually.

Mindful eating practices:

Portion control is not just about what you eat but also how you eat. Embracing mindful eating practices can enhance your awareness and help you savor every bite.

- • Slow down: Take your time to fully experience the flavors, textures, and aromas of your food. This can help you recognize feelings of fullness more easily.
- Use smaller plates: Opt for smaller plates or bowls, which can create a visual illusion of fuller portions and prevent overeating.
- Remove distractions: Avoid eating in front of screens or while multitasking, as these distractions can lead to mindless overeating.
- Practice Meal Prepping: Prepare and portion out meals and snacks in advance, making it easier to stick to appropriate serving sizes throughout the day.

Dining Out Strategies:

Navigating portion sizes when dining out can be challenging, but with a few smart strategies, you can enjoy restaurant meals while maintaining control.

- • Split a Main Dish: Share a larger entrée with a dining companion or ask for a portion to be packed for leftovers before it's served.
- Order Appetizers as Mains: Many appetizer portions can make for a satisfying main course, allowing you to indulge without overindulging.
- Request Half Portions or Side Salads: Inquire about options for smaller portions or consider replacing high-carb sides with a fresh salad.

Planning and preparation:

Proper planning and preparation can significantly improve your ability to maintain portion control throughout the week.

- Stock Up on Portion-Friendly Foods: Fill your pantry and fridge with single-serving or pre-portioned snacks and meals, reducing the temptation to overindulge.

- Meal Prep in Advance: Dedicate time each week to preparing and portioning out meals and snacks, making healthy choices more accessible.

- Stay Hydrated: Drink water or low-calorie beverages throughout the day to help manage hunger and prevent overeating.

Exercise and Activity Recommendations

Exercise and physical activity play a crucial role in managing diabetes and promoting overall well-being. Regular movement not only helps regulate blood sugar levels but also boosts energy, improves cardiovascular health, and enhances mood. By incorporating a variety of enjoyable activities into your routine, you can transform exercise from a chore into a rewarding and empowering experience.

When it comes to exercise for diabetes management, it's essential to strike a balance between aerobic activities, strength training, and flexibility exercises. This comprehensive approach will provide you with a well-rounded fitness regimen that addresses multiple aspects of your health.

Aerobic exercises, such as brisk walking, swimming, cycling, or dancing, are excellent choices for improving cardiovascular fitness and insulin sensitivity. These activities help your muscles utilize glucose more efficiently, which can lead to better blood sugar control. Aim for at least 150 minutes of moderate aerobic activity or 75 minutes of vigorous aerobic activity per week, spread out over several days.

Strength training, or resistance exercises, should also be a part of your routine. These activities, which can include weightlifting, resistance bands, or bodyweight exercises, help build and maintain lean muscle mass. Muscle tissue is more effective at utilizing glucose than fat tissue, which means that having more muscle can improve your body's ability to manage blood sugar levels. Aim for two to three strength training sessions per week, targeting all major muscle groups.

Flexibility and balance exercises, such as yoga, Pilates, or tai chi, offer numerous benefits for individuals with diabetes. These practices can improve range of motion, reduce stress and tension, and enhance balance and stability, which is particularly important for those at risk of complications like neuropathy. Incorporate flexibility exercises into your routine at least two to three times per week.

When embarking on a new exercise routine, it's crucial to start slowly and gradually increase the intensity and duration of your workouts. This approach will help you avoid injury and ensure a sustainable commitment to physical activity. Additionally, consulting with a healthcare professional or a certified fitness trainer can help you develop a personalized exercise plan tailored to your specific needs and fitness level.

Experiment with different activities and find those that you genuinely enjoy. Whether it's dancing, hiking, swimming, or playing a sport, engaging in activities you love will make exercise feel less like a chore and more like a rewarding part of your lifestyle.

Lastly, don't forget to stay hydrated, monitor your blood sugar levels before, during, and after exercise, and adjust your medication or insulin dosage as needed in consultation with your healthcare provider. By embracing physical activity and making it a priority, you'll not only better manage your diabetes but also experience a profound improvement in your overall quality of life.

Managing Stress and Emotional Eating

Stress and emotional eating are intertwined challenges that can significantly impact an individual's journey towards better health, especially for those managing diabetes. When emotions run high, the temptation to seek comfort in food can become overwhelming, potentially derailing even the most well-intentioned dietary plans. However, by developing a comprehensive toolkit of coping strategies and mindful techniques, you can regain control and cultivate a healthier relationship with food, effectively mitigating the risks associated with emotional eating.

At the core of managing emotional eating lies the ability to recognize and acknowledge the underlying emotions that trigger the urge to indulge. Whether it's anxiety, sadness, boredom, or even joy, these emotions can inadvertently lead to mindless snacking or overindulging. By taking a moment to pause and identify the emotion, you can then consciously choose a more constructive coping mechanism that aligns with your health goals.

One powerful tool in your arsenal is the practice of mindful eating. Instead of mindlessly consuming food while distracted by external stimuli, mindful eating encourages you to savor each bite, appreciating the flavors, textures, and sensations that accompany the experience. This heightened awareness can help you tune into your body's hunger and satiety cues, preventing overeating and fostering a more intuitive relationship with food.

Engaging in stress-relieving activities can also serve as a potent antidote to emotional eating. Regular exercise, whether it's a brisk walk, a yoga session, or dancing to your favorite tunes, can release endorphins and promote a sense of calm and well-being, reducing the urge to seek comfort in unhealthy food choices. Additionally, exploring hobbies, practicing relaxation techniques like deep breathing or meditation, or engaging in creative pursuits can provide a healthy outlet for managing stress and emotions.

Building a strong support system is another crucial component in combating emotional eating. Surrounding yourself with individuals who understand and encourage your journey can provide invaluable emotional support and accountability. Consider joining a support group, enlisting the help of a therapist, or confiding in a trusted friend or family member who can offer a listening ear and encouragement during challenging times.

Furthermore, it's essential to cultivate self-compassion and avoid the trap of harsh self-criticism. Emotional eating is a common struggle, and berating yourself for lapses or setbacks can only exacerbate the emotional turmoil and perpetuate the cycle. Instead, practice self-kindness, forgiveness, and a growth mindset, recognizing that each stumble is an opportunity to learn and refine your coping strategies.

Lastly, remember that managing emotional eating is an ongoing journey, and setbacks are inevitable. However, by embracing a holistic approach that addresses both the physical and emotional aspects of your well-being, you can cultivate a healthier relationship with food and develop resilience in the face of stress and emotional challenges, ultimately empowering you to lead a more balanced and fulfilling life while effectively managing your diabetes.

The Complete Diabetic Cookbook for Beginners

AUDIOBOOK

Scan the QR CODE and listen to the audiobook

Jarrell Knox

The Complete Diabetic Cookbook for Beginners

3 EBOOK BONUS

Scan the QR CODE and receive the 3 bonus ebooks. These ebooks can be useful for your friends or family to get extra information

http://subscribepage.io/01tYl3

Jarrell Knox

AUTHOR BIO

JARRELL KNOX

Raised in a tight-knit community, Knox developed an early affinity for the transformative potential of food. His formative years were spent in the kitchen alongside his grandmother, who instilled in him the significance of fresh ingredients and homemade meals. These experiences sparked a lifelong love affair with cooking.

Knox's path took an unexpected turn when a family member was diagnosed with diabetes. Motivated to make a positive impact, he delved into researching the disease and its intricate relationship with diet. Drawing upon his culinary expertise and extensive knowledge, Knox set out to create a cookbook that would empower individuals with diabetes to embrace flavorful, nourishing meals without compromising on taste or variety.

Beyond his literary achievements, Knox revels in his role as a devoted family man. He attributes his wife and children as the driving forces behind his writing journey, offering unwavering support and inspiration. Their presence fuels his relentless pursuit of creating accessible and enjoyable recipes that cater to the diverse needs of individuals and families affected by diabetes.

Printed in Great Britain
by Amazon